Little Prince, Little Prince, What Will You Be?

NAOMI ZACHARIAS

ART BY MARY EAKIN

HARVEST
kids

HARVEST HOUSE PUBLISHERS
EUGENE, OREGON

To Nico, my little prince behind the story

And to Jude, Isabella, and Jameson

Together you have given me a kingdom beyond my dreams

Illustrations and Design by Mary Eakin
Author photo by Elizabeth Jones

HARVEST KIDS is a trademark of The Hawkins Children's LLC.
Harvest House Publishers, Inc., is the exclusive licensee of the
trademark HARVEST KIDS.

Little Prince, Little Prince
Copyright © 2020 by Naomi Zacharias
Published by Harvest House Publishers
Eugene, Oregon 97408
www.harvesthousepublishers.com

ISBN 978-0-7369-7946-7 (hardcover)

Library of Congress Cataloging-in-Publication Data Record is avail-
able at https://lccn.loc.gov/2019054618.

Printed in China

21 22 23 24 25 26 27 28 / LP / 10 9 8 7 6 5 4

Little prince, little prince,
I wonder what you'll be.

I don't know the answer...

I'll have to wait and see.

If you are a waiter,

I'll eat out every night.

I'll order all the specials;
I'll swallow every bite!

Little prince, little prince,
I wonder what you'll be.

If you are a **teacher**,

I'll relearn my ABC's.

If you are a doctor,

appointments I will make.

I'm just sure that you would find

a cure for every ache.

If you are an **artist**,

I'll buy each work you do.

My house is
your museum,

a showcase
just for you.

Little prince, little prince,
I wonder what you'll be.

Jesus knows the answer...
I'll trust and wait and see.

He will be your strength,
He will be your guide,

He will mend each hurt and break,
Your heart He'll live inside.

You are his grandest masterpiece;
He couldn't love you more.

You're the work of God Himself...

Trust this, and you will soar.

Little prince, little prince,
I wonder what you'll be.

I don't know the answer...
I'll have to wait and see.

But this one thing I know for sure:
I'll be your biggest fan.

My heart will **always** flow with love

for you—my little man.

About the Author

Naomi Zacharias graduated from Wheaton College with a BA in Business/Economics. She is the director of Wellspring International, the humanitarian arm of RZIM. Naomi has visited women in red-light districts across Europe and Asia, foster homes for children affected by HIV/AIDS throughout Asia and Africa, displacement camps in Uganda, areas of the Middle East offering aid to Iraqi refugees, areas devastated by natural disaster, and international shelters for victims of human trafficking and domestic violence.

Naomi contributed a chapter on women and education in *Zealous Love: A Practical Guide to Social Justice*. She contributed two essays in the *NIV Bible for Women* and two essays in the *in(courage) Devotional Bible*. Naomi is one of six speakers featured on the *Real Women, Real Faith* DVDs and is the author of *The Scent of Water: Grace for Every Kind of Broken*.

Naomi lives in Atlanta, Georgia, with her family.